lonely planet

M

KUALA LUMPUR

1. FLIP

FLIP through the activity cards for morning, afternoon and evening.

2. MATCH

CHOOSE your day's itinerary by mixing and matching the cards.

3. GO

EVERYTHING you need for your city adventure is now at your fingertips.

MORNING

1. Petronas Towers
2. Merdeka Square
3. National Museum
4. Menara Kuala Lumpur
5. Bazaar Baru Chow Kit
6. Sri Mahamariamman Temple
7. Tun Abdul Razak Heritage Park
8. Batu Caves
9. Masjid Jamek
10. Thean Hou Temple
11. FRIM
12. Imbi Market
13. Bangsar Village I & II

AFTERNOON

14. NVAG
15. Spa Village
16. Rebung
17. KL Forest Eco Park
18. Kampung Baru
19. Starhill Culinary Studio
20. Central Market
21. Sultan Abdul Samad Building
22. Pavilion KL
23. Publika
24. Islamic Arts Museum
25. ILHAM
26. Afternoon Tea

EVENING

27. Jalan Alor
28. KLCC Park
29. No Black Tie
30. Glutton Street
31. Panggung Bandaraya
32. Chinatown
33. Omakase + Appreciate
34. Performing Arts Centre
35. Masjid India Pasar Malam
36. Buddhist Maha Vihara
37. Changkat Bukit Bintang
38. Kuala Lumpur Night Walk
39. TREC

FIND THE
KUALA LUMPU

Resembling two silver rockets preparing for take-off, the twin towers of Kuala Lumpur's iconic landmark are the perfect allegory for the meteoric rise of the city from tin-miners' hovel to 21st-century metropolis. The magnificent stainless steel skyscrapers are the crowning glory of the KLCC. (www.petronastwintowers.com.my; Jln Ampang; 9am-9pm Tue-Sun, closed 1-2.30pm Fri; KLCC)

★ **Top tip** Go early for the best views. Mornings in KL t... clearer than afterno... or be h...

Acros... ...ue K is ...uermama (ground flr, Ave K, 156 Jln Ampang; 10am-9.30pm), selling tasty Malaysian food.

MORNING

From here to yo... afternoon destination

15min 20min 20min 15... 15min 25min 20min 35min 20min 25min 45min 30min 30min

...e Nationa... ...l Arts Gallery showcases contemporary Malaysian art. There are often interesting temporary shows of local and regional artists, as well as pieces from the gallery's permanent collection of 4000 works. There are seven galleries in total including the Reka Gallery, with pieces related to industrial design, architecture and fashion. (NVAG; 2 Jln Temerloh; 10am-6pm; Titiwangsa)

★ **Don't miss** renowned batik artist Chuah Thean Teng's *Perairan Pulau Pinang*.

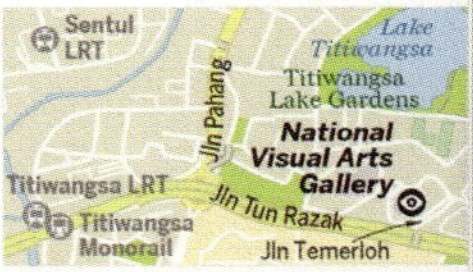

For self-service Malay and mamak fare head to the **D'Istana Jalamas Café** (Jln Tun Razak; 7am-8pm Mon-Fri) at the Istana Budaya.

AFTERN...

From here to your evening destination

25min 20min 20min 20min 35min 15min 15min 15min 15min 20min 20min 40min 15min

The collection of roadside restaurants and stalls lining Jln Alor hauls in everyone from sequinned society babes to penny-strapped backpackers. From around 5pm till late every evening, the street transforms into a continuous open-air dining space with hundreds of plastic tables and chairs and rival caterers shouting out to passers-by to drum up business (avoid the pushiest ones!). Most places serve alcohol and you can sample pretty much every Malay Chinese dish imaginable, from grilled fish and satay to Chinese greens and fried noodles with frogs' legs. (24hr; AirAsia-Bukit Bintang)

Wong Ah Wah (1-9 Jln Alor; 5pm-4am) is unbeatable for addictive spicy chicken wings, as well as grilled seafood, tofu and satay.

EVENING

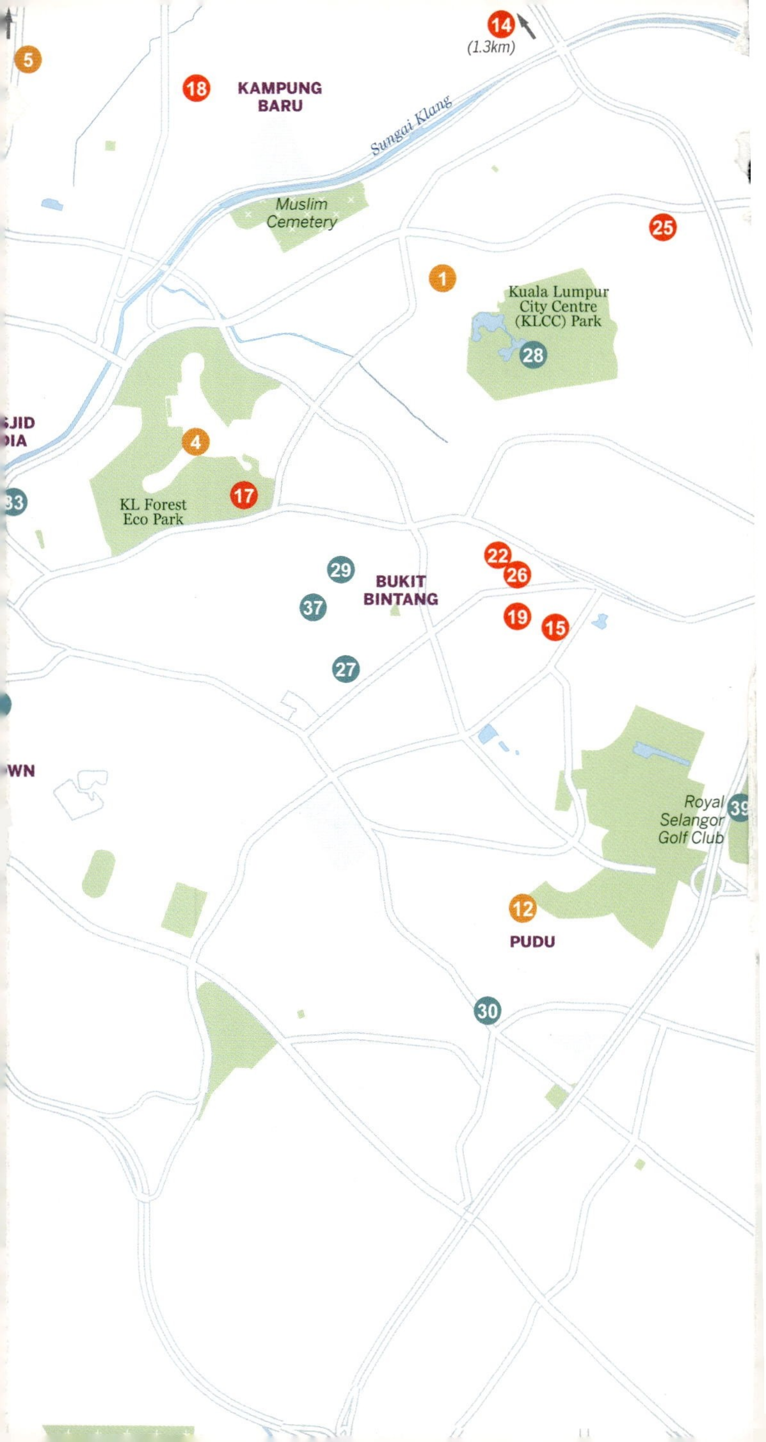
14
(1.3km)
5
18
KAMPUNG BARU
Sungai Klang
Muslim Cemetery
25
1
Kuala Lumpur City Centre (KLCC) Park
28
4
17
KL Forest Eco Park
29
BUKIT BINTANG
22
26
37
19
15
27
Royal Selangor Golf Club
12
PUDU
30

BEST OF
JR, QUICKLY.

The transport planner shows you how long it takes to get from one activity to the next, by foot, train, bus, LRT or taxi.

Find the best and closest eating options to where you're enjoying your day.

Mini-maps help you get your bearings and show you the nearest transport stops.

Turn over for the fold-out map to help you plot your perfect day.

KUALA LUMPUR

PULL-OUT MAP AT BACK WITH TRANSIT MAP

These twin malls are linked by a covered bridge and offer upmarket fashions, including local designers such as Jonathan Liang at d.d.collective, Comoddity menswear by Vincent Siow, Fashion Valet specialising in Muslim fashion and TriBeCa for children's clothing and accessories. There's also a play centre for kids and the excellent Hammam Spa. (www.bangsarvillage.com; cnr Jln Telawi 1 & Jln Telawi 2, Bangsar Baru; 10am-10pm; M Bank Rakyat-Bangsar)

★ **Don't miss** Silverfish Books is also a publisher of Malaysian literature and hosts regular talks.

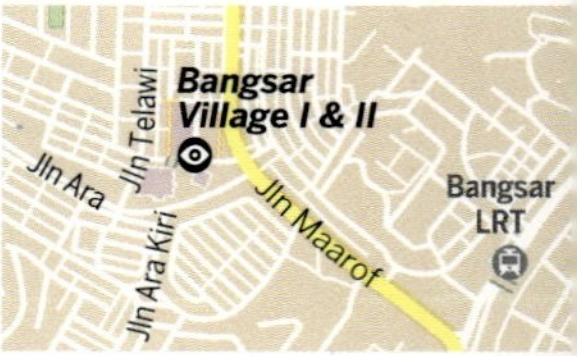

The closest thing to a Jewish deli in KL, **Nutmeg** (Bangsar Village II; 9.30am-10pm) makes an impression with its bagel and lox.

MORNING

From here to your afternoon destination

25min 20min 15min 25min 30min 20min 20min 30min 20min 20min 40min 25min 25min

The British left behind a strong attachment to afternoon tea, consumed here in the form of tea or coffee and a sweet or savoury snack such as *tong sui,* various Indian fritters, battered and fried slices of cassava, sweet potato, banana and – of course – *kueh* (traditional cakes often made from glutinous rice). **TWG Tea** (www.twgtea.com; level 2, Pavilion KL, 168 Jln Bukit Bintang; AirAsia-Bukit Bintang) offers a mind-boggling range of more than 400 teas and infusions. The teas are beautifully packaged for gifts, too. It serves afternoon tea daily (2pm to 6pm).

Don't miss the delectable tea-infused macarons at **TWG Tea** – flavours include Earl Grey and chocolate.

From here to your evening destination

10min 10min 25min 10min 15min 15min 15min 20min 10min 20min 15min 15min 10min

This new entertainment complex is home to a variety of bars, eateries and venues for live music and comedy, including COMO (www.facebook.com/comokl/), a great spot for Spanish tapas, expertly mixed cocktails and live music. TREC is also home to superclub **Zouk** (www.zoukclub.com.my), which has seven interlinked DJ spaces, and **Live House** (www.facebook.com/livehousekl), an excellent new live music and comedy venue on the Electric Blvd. (www.trec.com.my; 436 Jln Tun Razak; AirAsia-Bukit Bintang)

As well as gigs, **Live House** also offers tasty Southern-style soul food (fried chicken, burgers and wraps).

GETTING AROUND

LIGHT RAIL TRANSIT (LRT)

Rapid KL runs the **Light Rail Transit system** (LRT; 03-7885 2585; www.myrapid.com.my; from RM1.30; every 6-10min 6am-11.45pm Mon-Sat, to 11.30pm Sun). There are three lines: the Ampang line from Ampang to Sentul Timur; the Sri Petaling line from Sentul Timur to Putra Heights; and the Kelana Jaya line from Gombak to Putra Heights. The network is poorly integrated because the lines were constructed by different companies. As a result, you may have to follow a series of walkways, stairs and elevators, or walk several blocks down the street.

MONORAIL

The air-conditioned **monorail** (www.myrapid.com.my; RM1.20-4.10; 6am-midnight) zips from KL Sentral to Titiwangsa, linking many of the city's sightseeing areas.

TICKETS & PASSES

Rapid KL offers the **MyRapid** (www.myrapid.com.my) pre-paid card, valid on Rapid KL buses, the monorail and the Ampang and Kelana Jaya LRT lines. It costs RM20 (including RM5 in credit) and can be bought at monorail and LRT stations. Just tap at the ticket gates or when you get on the bus and the correct fare will be deducted.

The **Touch 'n Go card** (www.touchngo.com.my) can be used on all public transport. The cards, which cost RM10.60 and can be reloaded with values from RM10 to RM500, can be purchased at KL Sentral and the central LRT stations KLCC, Masjid Jamek and Dang Wangi.

For short-term stays you are better off buying individual tickets. Buy single-journey tokens from the cashier or electronic ticket machines.

FROM THE AIRPORTS

KUL

Kuala Lumpur International Airport (KLIA) is about 55km south of the city.

- Airport Coach, RM18, 1 hour to KL Sentral
- fixed-fare coupons from RM75, 1 hour
- KLIA Ekspres, RM55, fastest way to the city

SZB

SkyPark Subang Airport is around 20km west of the city.

- Trans MVS Express, RM10, 1 hour to KL Sentral
- RM40 to RM50, traffic can be heavy

OTHER TRANSPORT

Free bus The GO-KL free city bus has four circular routes around the city, with stops at KLCC, KL Tower, KL Sentral, the National Museum and Merdeka Sq. Buses run every five minutes during peak hours and every 10 to 15 minutes at other times.

Taxis KL has plenty of air-conditioned taxis, which queue up at designated taxi stops across the city. You can flag down moving taxis, but drivers will stop only if there is a convenient place to pull over. Fares start at RM3 for the first three minutes, with an additional 25 sen for each 36 seconds. From midnight to 6am there's a surcharge of 50% on the metered fare, and extra passengers (more than two) add 20 sen each to the starting fare. Blue taxis are newer and more comfortable and start at RM6 for the first three minutes and RM1 for each additional 36 seconds. Night surcharges of 50% also apply.

Unfortunately, some drivers have limited geographical knowledge of the city. Some also refuse to use the meter, even though this is a legal requirement. Note that KL Sentral and some large malls such as Pavilion and Suria KLCC have a coupon system for taxis where you pay in advance at a slightly higher fee than the meter.

One of the easiest ways to use taxis in KL is to download an app such as Uber, Easy Taxi or Grab (formally known as My Teksi) to your smartphone or tablet.

SHOPPING

SHOP FOR YOURSELF

Skilled artisans may be a dying breed, but you can still find great handmade craft items for sale in KL. Fashion outlets, contemporary-art galleries, antique stores and interior-design shops are also worth a look.

Counterfeit goods are a problem – not just Prada handbags and Rolex watches but also software and electronics. Buyer beware!

KL is liberally peppered with air-conditioned malls, such as Publika and Pavilion KL. Some are so big it would take several days to do them justice.

Major fashion labels with outlets in KL include British India (at Pavilion KL, Bangsar Village and Publika), which sells high-quality linen and cotton pieces, and Bonia, which offers Italian-style leather fashions and accessories.

SHOP FOR OTHERS

Objects crafted out of pewter are synonymous with Selangor. Royal Selangor has several outlets in major malls, including Suria KLCC and Pavilion KL.

Eye-catching *wayang kulit* (shadow puppets) are made from buffalo hide to portray characters from epic Hindu legends, while kites are made from paper and bamboo strips in a variety of traditional designs. The crescent-shaped *wau bulan* (moon kite) can reach 3m in length and breadth, while the *wau kucing* (cat kite) is the logo of Malaysia Airlines. You can find kites and puppets in Central Market.

SHOP FOR KIDS

At Avenue K, don't miss the interactive dinosaur exhibition Discoveria (www.discoveria.com.my). Publika has a particularly good selection of shops for kids and parents. Megakidz in Mid Valley Megamall and Kizsport & Gym in Bangsar Village II have play spaces and crèches.

Older kids and teens will love exploring the warren of youth-oriented outlets at Sungei Wang Plaza. The Tokyo Street section of Pavilion KL is also a dream for those into Japanese fashion and comic cultures.

NEED TO KNOW

MONEY

Currency The ringgit (RM) is made up of 100 sen. Coins in use are one sen, five sen, 10 sen, 20 sen and 50 sen; notes are RM1, RM5, RM10, RM50 and RM100.

TIPPING

0% (taxi) 0-10% (restaurant)

Tipping Not generally expected, but leaving small change in a cafe or restaurant is appreciated. Many restaurants in KL add a service charge of around 10% onto the bill.

ATMs & credit cards ATMs widely available; credit cards accepted in most hotels and restaurants.

OPENING HOURS

- Restaurants Noon to 2.30pm and 6pm to 10.30pm
- Shops 9.30am to 7pm Monday to Saturday, malls 10am to 10pm daily

WEBSITES

Visit KL (www.visitkl.gov.my) Official city tourism site.

Time Out KL (www.timeoutkl.com) Monthly listings magazine with an excellent website.

Zafigo (http://zafigo.com) Specialises in advice for women travellers in the region.

Lonely Planet (www.lonelyplanet.com/malaysia/kuala-lumpur) Destination information, hotel bookings, traveller forum and more.

DOS & DON'TS

- ✓ Take off your shoes Always remove your footwear before entering someone's home.
- ✓ Use your right hand Use your right hand to eat, in shops, when shaking hands or for any other transaction. The left hand is reserved for unclean acts.
- ✗ Don't point with your index finger Use your thumb instead.

IF YOU LIKE...

LOCAL LIFE

Breakfast with the locals at 5 Bazaar Baru Chow Kit, one of KL's most atmospheric wet markets. In the afternoon, head to 18 Kampung Baru to experience a Malay village in the centre of the city. End your day at 30 Glutton Street, an alley lined with hawker stalls, to dine like a local.

FREE STUFF

Stroll around 2 Merdeka Square, the place where Malaysian independence was declared, and admire the colonial architecture. Spend the afternoon viewing the latest exhibition of Malaysian art at 25 ILHAM. Once the sun has gone down, join the crowds in 28 KLCC Park to watch the Petronas Towers light up and catch the Lake Symphony fountains play.

FAMILY ACTIVITIES

Visit the 7 Tun Abdul Razak Heritage Park, which is home to a bird park, a planetarium and a butterfly park. Kids will also enjoy traversing canopy walkways through the jungle at 17 KL Forest Eco Park. There are plenty of dishes to try at the evening hawker market, 27 Jalan Alor, from the adventurous to the more familiar.

TRIP PLANNER

DAY 1

MORNING

AFTERNOON

EVENING

DAY 2

MORNING

AFTERNOON

EVENING

DAY 3

MORNING

AFTERNOON

EVENING

NOTES

NOTES

NOTES

BEHIND THE SCENES

SEND US YOUR FEEDBACK

We love to hear from travellers – your comments help make our books better. Visit lonelyplanet.com/contact to submit your updates and suggestions.

ACKNOWLEDGMENTS

Thanks to

Lonely Planet's Kuala Lumpur writer: Isabel Albiston
Product editor: Kate Mathews
Assisting editor: Kate James
Senior cartographer: Julie Sheridan
Book designer: Jessica Rose
Cartographers: Mark Griffiths, Valentina Kremenchutskaya

Thanks to: Indra Kilfoyle, Anne Mason, Rick Wiebusch

Images: 1 Papa Annur/Shutterstock ©; 2 Tom Bonaventure/Getty Images ©; 3 JSvideos/Shutterstock ©; 4 Victor Maschek/Shutterstock ©; 5 Gwoeii/Shutterstock ©; 6 Amble Design/Shutterstock ©; 7 Zhukova Valentyna/Shutterstock ©; 8 Jarel Remick/500px ©; 9 NaughtyNut/Shutterstock ©; 10 WEKWEK/Getty Images ©; 11 Hanafi Latif/Shutterstock ©; 12 Andrew TB Tan/Getty Images ©; 13 Inmagineasia/Getty Images ©; 14 Image courtesy of National Visual Art Gallery (NVAG) ©; 15 Alena Ozerova/Shutterstock ©; 16 Kelvin Wong/Shutterstock ©; 17 Zuhairi Ahmad/Shutterstock ©; 18 Tom Bryan/Getty Images ©; 19 JoannaTkaczuk/Shutterstock ©; 20 NURUL AINI/Shutterstock ©; 21 gracethang2/Shutterstock ©; 22 Takashi Images/Shutterstock ©; 23 Calvin Chan/Shutterstock ©; 24 Alizada Studios/Shutterstock ©; 25 Image courtesy of IHLAM ©; 26 ThamKC/Shutterstock ©; 27 Migel/Shutterstock ©; 28 Sean Pavone/Getty Images ©; 29 PeopleImages.com/Getty Images ©; 30 Calvin Chan/Shutterstock ©; 31 Dmitry Petrenko/Shutterstock ©; 32 Elena Ermakova/Shutterstock ©; 33 JGI/Jamie Grill/Getty Images ©; 34 Image courtesy of the Kuala Lumpur Performing Arts Centre (klpac) ©; 35 HUZAIME/Shutterstock ©; 36 udeyismail/Shutterstock ©; 37 MarkD800/Getty Images ©; 38 f11photo/Shutterstock ©; 39 Pressmaster/Shutterstock ©; (top to bottom) Getting Around: Aizuddin Saad/Shutterstock ©; Avesun/Shutterstock ©; Shopping: Johan Design Associates/Getty Images ©; buttet/Shutterstock ©; Need to Know: kenary820/Shutterstock ©

Cover images: (top to bottom) Sunrise over Kuala Lumpur, BlackCat Imaging/Shutterstock ©; Thean Hou Temple, Gavin Hellier/AWL ©; Merdeka Square, fotoVoyager/Getty ©

OUR STORY

A beat-up old car, a few dollars in the pocket and a sense of adventure. In 1972 that's all Tony and Maureen Wheeler needed for the trip of a lifetime – across Europe and Asia overland to Australia. It took several months, and at the end – broke but inspired – they sat at their kitchen table writing and stapling together their first travel guide, *Across Asia on the Cheap*. Within a week they'd sold 1500 copies. Lonely Planet was born. Today, Lonely Planet has offices in Melbourne, London and Oakland, with more than 600 staff and writers. We share Tony's belief that 'a great guidebook should do three things: inform, educate and amuse'.

GET THE RIGHT GUIDES FOR YOUR TRIP

COUNTRY, CITY & REGIONAL
- The original
- Comprehensive

PHRASEBOOK

POCKET
- Pocket-sized
- Easy-to-use

LOOKING FOR OTHER TRAVEL RESOURCES?

LONELYPLANET.COM
For travel information, advice, tips & digital chapters

EBOOKS
Guidebooks for your reader
lonelyplanet.com/ebooks

MAGAZINE
For travel stories, inspiration & ideas
lonelyplanet.com/magazine

STAY IN TOUCH

lonelyplanet.com/contact

AUSTRALIA Levels 2 & 3, 551 Swanston Street, Carlton, Vic 3053
☎ 03 8379 8000 **FAX** 03 8379 8111

EUROPE Unit E, Digital Court, The Digital Hub, Rainsford St, Dublin 8, Ireland

USA 124 Linden St, Oakland, CA 94607
☎ 510 250 6400 **TOLL FREE** 800 275 8555 **FAX** 510 893 8572

UK 240 Blackfriars Rd, London SE1 8NW
☎ 020 3771 5100 **FAX** 020 3771 5101

twitter.com/lonelyplanet
facebook.com/lonelyplanet
instagram.com/lonelyplanet
youtube.com/lonelyplanet
lonelyplanet.com/newsletter

Published by

Lonely Planet Global Limited
CRN 554153

Levels 2 & 3, 551 Swanston Street, Carlton, Victoria 3053, Australia

1st edition July 2017

10 9 8 7 6 5 4 3 2 1

Printed in China

FSC www.fsc.org MIX Paper from responsible sources FSC™ C021741

Paper in this book is certified against the Forest Stewardship Council™ standards. FSC™ promotes environmentally responsible, socially beneficial and economically viable management of the world's forests.

LONELY PLANET'S

3 PERFECT DAYS

DAY 1

1 PETRONAS TOWERS Prebook tickets to go up the towers for views over KL.

25 ILHAM Take a look at contemporary Malaysian art in the Foster + Partners–designed tower.

32 CHINATOWN Push your way through the crowds at the Petaling Street Market.

DAY 2

2 MERDEKA SQUARE Admire the square's historic buildings and colonial architecture.

17 KL FOREST ECO PARK Traverse the park's canopy walkway.

27 JALAN ALOR Sample an array of street food from the stalls and restaurants.

DAY 3

8 BATU CAVES Head just out of the city to this iconic Hindu shrine in a limestone cave.

24 ISLAMIC ARTS MUSEUM View the splendid collection of Islamic decorative arts.

33 OMAKASE + APPRECIATE Pop in for a cocktail at this speakeasy-style bar.

1 PETRONAS TOWERS

KL's iconic twin skyscrapers

14 NVAG

Malaysia's top fine-art collection

27 JALAN ALOR

Tasty dishes and cold beer